Whale Tales

story and photographs by

Kim Westerskov

Learning Media

Contents

1. Getting to Know Whales 3

2. Orca – Killer Whales 10

3. A Birthday Whale 17

4. Humpback Whales 22

5. Cuddled by a Whale 26

   The Whales in this Book 32

1.
Getting to Know Whales

I love whales and dolphins. They are wonderful animals to be with – when I can find them! The ocean is a big place, and often even whales just seem to "disappear" in it.

If I'm in the right place at the right time,
whales can be easy to find. But sometimes
I look out at the empty ocean, day after day.
It's fun trying to find whales, though – and
it's very exciting when I do find them.
Let me tell you some of these whale tales.

My job is to take photographs of the sea
and its animals. Usually, whales don't want me
to come too close to them.

**Whales and dolphins are mammals like
us. They breathe air, they have warm
blood, and they give birth to live babies
which are fed on mother's milk.**

**There are about forty kinds of whales.
Some are huge – the blue whale can be
100 feet long and weigh up to 200 tons.
The dwarf sperm whale doesn't grow
longer than 9 feet and weighs up to about
450 pounds. That's smaller than some of
the big dolphins.**

But sometimes, a whale will come to have a closer look at *me*. Times like that can be very exciting – or very scary! When I'm with whales, and the sea isn't too rough, I think I have the best job in the world.

This small minke whale stayed
near our yacht for hours. The water wasn't very
clear, but I got into my wet suit and hopped in.
The minke swam round me for about an hour.
It got closer and closer. Then it swam right
under me and disappeared.

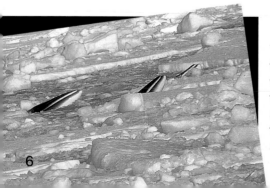

The minke whale is
found in most of the
world's oceans. These
three minke whales
are coming up
through the broken
sea ice to breathe.

Sperm whales are huge.
If the water is not clear, it's hard to see the
whole whale at one time. When I've dived with
sperm whales, the water has always been dirty.
All I could see was part of the whale – a tail,
a head, or a body slowly moving past.

The sperm whale is the largest predator ever to have
lived on earth – much bigger than Tyrannosaurus Rex.
But sperm whales are gentle with people – unless you
throw a harpoon into them! They are champion divers,
and they can hold their breath for up to two hours.

The fin whale is the second longest of all the whales. Only the mighty blue whale is bigger. We followed a group of fin whales for over an hour. One of them swam right in front of the boat, like dolphins do. This is called "bowriding." I wanted to get into the water with the fin whales, but they were moving too fast and were never on the surface for very long.

Here, two dusky dolphins are swimming very close to me. I could have reached out and touched them – but I don't usually touch animals unless they want to touch me.

Floating in clear, blue sea with playful dolphins is a wonderful experience.

9

2.
Orca – Killer Whales

Orca, or killer whales, are sometimes called the "wolves of the sea." They live and hunt in groups called "pods." Orca eat all kinds of sea animals, even other whales, but they leave people alone.

An orca has never attacked a human in the ocean. In fact, orca are gentle with people.

Sometimes orca pop their heads out of the water to see what is happening up above. This is called "spy hopping." Once, I was standing on the ice in Antarctica when three orca came up out of the sea right in front of me.

There are stories of orca sneaking up behind divers and gently grabbing hold of their flippers or legs. For the orca this is "playing," but it usually gives the diver a big fright.

Once, I saw a pod of orca playing with this large shark – just like a cat plays with a mouse. Sometimes, an orca would slap the sea very hard with its tail, right next to the shark's head. The shark didn't seem very happy about this. I wanted to swim with orca, but I didn't think that was the best time to try.

A few years later, I had another chance. I have a friend who takes people dolphin-watching on his yacht. I was sailing with him one day, and we knew there were orca nearby. It was a calm day, but it still took us quite a while to find them.

One orca swam slowly past us on its side. It was having a good look at us. I knew that some people think orca are gentle and wouldn't hurt a human in the water. But I'm about the same size as a seal or dolphin – and orca eat seals and dolphins! If one of these whales wanted to hurt me, I couldn't do much to stop it.

There was a lot to think about, but if I was going to swim with orca, today was the day. I got my underwater camera ready. I put my wet suit on and slipped quietly into the water. We were a few miles out to sea, and the water was dirty. I stayed on the surface and looked for killer whale fins. I felt very small and very alone.

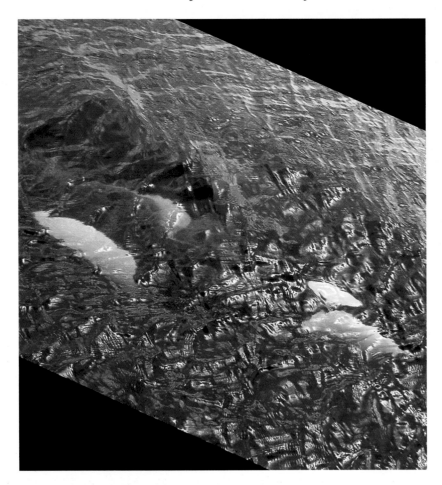

Suddenly there they were – three of them, swimming straight toward me. Underwater, everything looks bigger than it really is, and orca are big to begin with. I don't get scared in the sea very often, but now I was scared.

They looked so powerful – their size, the huge jaws, and those teeth! I could see the teeth of the middle whale as it swam past. Something white was hanging from its mouth. Later, when I looked at my photos, I saw that it was a stingray that the orca was carrying.

When I was safely back on the boat, I realized how frightened I was. I was shaking. The orca hadn't done anything to frighten me – they were just so big and powerful.

I swam with the orca many more times that day. After a while, I stopped being scared.

I started to really like these whales.

3.
A Birthday Whale

The right whale was the first large whale to be hunted by people. Whalers named it the right whale because it was the "right" whale to catch – it is a slow swimmer, it floats when it has been killed, and it gives a lot of oil and good whalebone. Over 100 000 right whales were killed last century. Now there are only a few thousand right whales left in the world's oceans.

Once, I was diving near the Auckland Islands, taking photos of southern right whales. We were there for three weeks, so I made dozens of dives, but the day I remember was 26 July – my 50th birthday.

I knew it was going to be a good day. What I didn't know was that it would be one of the best days of my life. We drove our inflatable boat to the eastern end of one of the islands. There were whales there that day, the water looked clear, and the sea was calm.

The right whale looks quite different to all other whales. It is a fat, black whale with no back fin. It has a huge head covered with white or yellow lumps, called "callosities." This is my first underwater meeting with southern right whales. A mother and her calf swam slowly under me in the clear, cold water.

I put on my gear and checked my cameras, and then I slipped quietly over the side. The water was cold, clear … and empty. But not for long. On my right, a whale swam slowly toward me. Then, on my left, a huge whale swam toward the smaller one. I could see now that this was a mother and her calf. The mother was trying to keep the calf away from me. But this youngster wanted to know what was going on.

The baby swam up over its mom's back and kept coming toward me. By the time it got to me, it didn't look like a baby anymore. It was huge – at least fifteen feet long! If I had held out my hand, I could have touched it.

Then, as it slowly passed, I saw an eye peering at me. It seemed to be saying, "Who are you, and what are you doing here?" It was magical. Then baby and mother swam slowly off into the blue distance. Wow! What a birthday!

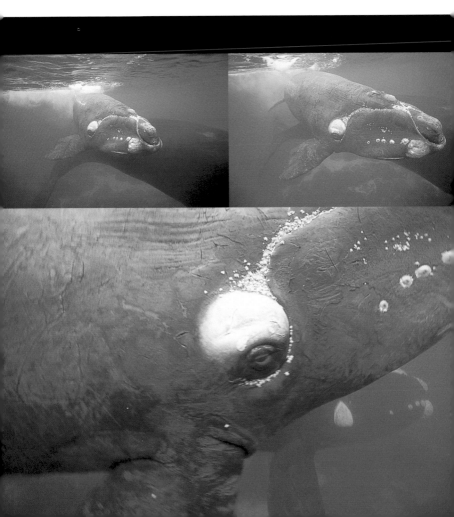

4.
Humpback Whales

Humpback whales are probably the best known of all the large whales. They have large, knobbly heads and huge flippers. They are famous for their songs – the longest and most complicated songs in the animal kingdom.

Thousands of people around the world watch the humpback from "whale-watch" boats. Many whales are hard to find, but not humpbacks. Every year, they go to the same breeding areas and stay there for many months. Humpbacks swim slowly, and they are the most interesting of all whales to watch.

Once, there were over 100 000 humpbacks in the southern seas alone. But the humpback was a favorite of the whalers – now there are only a few thousand humpbacks left.

Much of a whale's life happens underwater. But humpbacks spend a lot of time on the surface of the sea where we can watch them from boats or from the shore. They slap their heads, tails, and fins on the water. They "spy hop" and head butt. Sometimes, with two or three beats of its tail, the humpback whale will push its giant body up into the air, falling back with a tremendous splash.

Humpbacks live in all the world's oceans. In the summer, they are found at their feeding grounds in icy seas. By winter, they have migrated to warmer waters to breed. Over the years, I've spent many months with humpbacks.

5.
Cuddled by a Whale

My most awesome meeting with a humpback whale was in the warm, clear waters of the South Pacific Ocean. It was a beautiful day – there was no cloud or wind, and the water was clear. We knew that a mother and baby humpback were somewhere around, but we hadn't seen them for a while.

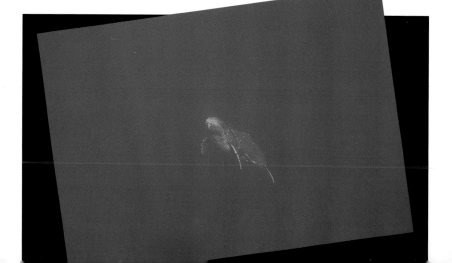

Then I saw the calf as it swam up through the dark blue water. It turned toward me, growing larger and larger. Its white skin seemed to glow. It passed so close that it almost touched me with its long flipper. Even though it was only a few weeks old, it was still about fifteen feet from nose to tail. It already weighed over a ton.

The whale swam past me and headed for my
buddy. What happened next? Well, my buddy
thinks he moved back because the whale was
too close for good photos. As I remember it,
the baby whale just bumped into him and
gently pushed him out of the way.

Then it swam back to me … closer and closer … until it bumped into me with its right flipper. It did this again, three or four times. It was probably a gentle bump for the baby whale, but to me it felt like I was being hit by a small truck.

Its long flipper was curved forwards, like it was cuddling me. Cuddling me? Whales don't cuddle humans! Well, maybe not, but that's what it felt like.

It was a moment of wonder. We were looking into each other's eyes, less than two feet apart! What was the whale thinking? I have no idea. But I remember what *I* was thinking – "Wow! I'm so lucky!"

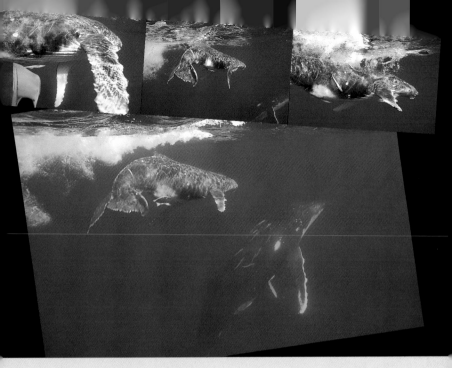

Then the mother whale arrived. The baby let go of me and slowly swam back to her.

Later I wondered, "Did I take any photos of the cuddle?" It all happened so quickly. It would have been very easy to forget to take any photos at all.

Weeks later, when I had the photos developed, I found that I **had** kept taking photos! It was good to look at them and remember what had happened.

Being cuddled by a whale was an amazing experience!

The Whales in this Book

 Orca grow to a length of 20 to 26 feet, and sometimes to over 30 feet. They can weigh from 3 to 6 tons, and occasionally up to 10 tons.

 The male sperm whale can grow to be over 60 feet long and weigh 50 tons, sometimes more.

 The right whale is one of the largest of all whales, reaching a length of 60 feet and a weight of 40 to 80 tons, sometimes up to 100 tons. Only the giant blue whale is heavier.

 Minke whales can grow up to 30 feet and weigh up to 8 tons, although some have weighed over 13 tons.

 Fin whales grow to an average length of around 70 feet. The largest ever measured was 88 feet. Adults weigh from 45 to 75 tons, depending on what time of year it is.

 The humpback whale grows to an average length of 50 feet, and occasionally up to 60 feet. Adults usually weigh 25 to 30 tons, sometimes reaching 50 tons – the weight of a herd of a dozen large elephants.

Note: Many countries have laws about how people should behave when they are around whales. You may have to get a special permit if you want to get close to them. Kim Westerskov had all the permits that were needed for the "whale tales" in this book.